WORKING AT THE POST OFFICE

by Katie Marsico

CHERRY LAKE PUBLISHING * ANN ARBOR, MICHIGAN

Published in the United States of America by Cherry Lake Publishing
Ann Arbor, Michigan
www.cherrylakepublishing.com

Content Adviser: Thad Dilley, U.S. Postal Service
Reading Adviser: Cecilia Minden-Cupp, PhD, Literacy Consultant

Photo Credits: Page 4, ©Jeff Greenberg/Alamy; page 6, ©Ted Pink/Alamy; cover and page 8, ©David R. Frazier Photolibrary, Inc./Alamy; page 10, ©iStockphoto.com/MichaelDeLeon; page 12, ©Dennis MacDonald/Alamy; cover and page 14, ©Copyright Canada Post Corporation; cover and page 16, ©Ellen Isaacs/Alamy; cover and page 18, ©Powered by Light/Alan Spencer/Alamy; page 20, ©iStockphoto.com/Juanmonino

LIBRARY OF CONGRESS CATALOGING-IN-PUBLICATION DATA
Marsico, Katie, 1980–
   Working at the post office / by Katie Marsico.
       p. cm.—(21st century junior library)
   Includes index.
   ISBN-13: 978-1-60279-512-9
   ISBN-10: 1-60279-512-6
   1. Postal service—Employees—Juvenile literature. 2. Postal
service—Juvenile literature. 3. Postal service—Juvenile literature.
I. Title.
   HE6078.M37 2010
   383'.4973023—dc22   2008045236

Cherry Lake Publishing would like to acknowledge the work of
The Partnership for 21st Century Skills.
Please visit www.21stcenturyskills.org for more information.

CONTENTS

Post office workers help many customers each day.

What Is a Post Office?

You are waiting in line. There are many people. Everyone is holding a letter or a **package**. Some people need to buy stamps. Other people have questions about the best way to send their mail. Where are you? You are at a post office!

The post office sells many different kinds of stamps.

People visit the post office to mail letters and ship packages. Maybe they are sending packages to friends who live far away. People buy boxes or stamps at the post office, too.

Have you ever wondered how mail gets to your house? It takes many people to get the mail to a worker who brings it to your home.

Some post office workers use machines.

There are many different jobs at the post office. **Postmasters** and **clerks** are two kinds of post office workers. These workers help you send and receive mail. Are you ready to learn more about post office workers?

Make a Guess!

Guess how many people work at your local post office. Write down your guess. Are you visiting the post office soon? Ask the clerk for an exact number of workers the next time you go. Was your guess correct?

A postmaster must be very organized. She must also be a good leader.

Post Office Workers

A postmaster runs your local post office. She is in charge of all the workers. The postmaster spends time talking to customers. She makes sure people can easily send and receive mail.

Good clerks are friendly. They are happy to answer customers' questions.

Clerks help the post office run smoothly, too. Some clerks work at the front of the post office. They stand behind the counter. They sell stamps and help customers. Clerks also answer questions about packages and letters.

Think!

Post office clerks weigh letters or packages on a scale. This lets customers know how much it costs to send the mail. Do you think it costs more to send big or heavy items? Why?

A Canadian mail carrier delivers mail to a customer. People all over the world get mail.

Other clerks and workers **sort** the mail. They use special machines to do this. These workers help make sure mail goes to the correct **mail carrier**.

Mail carriers deliver the mail. They bring letters and packages to the right addresses. Mail carriers also pick up mail from houses and mailboxes. They bring this mail back to the post office.

Is your post office neat and clean? Custodians help keep it that way.

Mail handlers unload the mail from post office trucks. These workers bring the mail inside the post office building. That is where it is sorted for delivery.

Mechanics fix and care for the sorting machines and the trucks. **Custodians** keep the post office clean. The post office has many workers. Each one wants to help you send and receive mail.

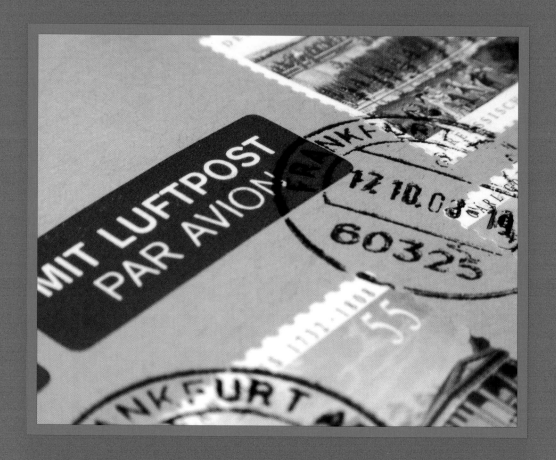

Post office workers handle mail from all over the world. This package was mailed from Germany.

Do You Want to Work at the Post Office?

Would you like a job at the post office someday? Talk to workers when you visit the post office. Find out what skills these people need to do their jobs.

You might learn that post office workers enjoy helping others. Most also pay close attention to details such as names and numbers.

Many workers help get your mail to your home.

How can you prepare for a job at the post office? Try sorting your family's mail every day. Bring each letter to the correct person.

A post office is a great place to work. Learn as much as you can now. This will help you decide if a post office job is right for you!

Ask Questions!

Ask your mail carrier about his job. How many hours each week does he spend delivering mail? What is the hardest part of the job? Asking questions will help you learn about jobs that interest you.

GLOSSARY

clerks (KLURKS) people who sort mail and help customers send letters and packages

custodians (kuhs-TOH-dee-uhnz) people who clean buildings such as the post office

mail carrier (MAYL KAIR-ee-ur) a person who delivers mail and picks up mail from mailboxes

mechanics (muh-KAN-iks) people who fix machines or make sure they are working correctly

package (PAK-ij) a box or container used to send something

postmasters (POHST-mass-turz) people in charge of post offices

sort (SORT) to separate or put things in a certain order

FIND OUT MORE

BOOKS

Bourgeois, Paulette. *Postal Workers.* Tonawanda, NY: Kids Can Press, 2005.

Trumbauer, Lisa. *What Does a Mail Carrier Do?* Berkeley Heights, NJ: Enslow Publishers, 2005.

WEB SITES

Ben's Guide to U.S. Government for Kids— Your Neighborhood: The Letter Carrier
bensguide.gpo.gov/k-2/ neighborhood/lettercarrier.html
Learn what a mail carrier does in your community

United States Postal Service
www.usps.com/
Check out stamps and learn more about the United States Postal Service

INDEX

ABOUT THE AUTHOR

Katie Marsico is the author of more than 40 children's books. She lives in Elmhurst, Illinois, with her husband and children. She would especially like to thank Timothy Ratliff of the U.S. Postal Service for helping her research this title.